D0644012

JUSTIN BIEBER

Kathleen Tracy

Mitchell Lane
PUBLISHERS

P.O. Box 196
Hockessin, Delaware 19707
Visit us on the web: www.mitchelllane.com
Comments? email us: mitchelllane@mitchelllane.com

Mitchell Lane
PUBLISHERS

Printing   2   3   4   5   6   7   8   9

A Robbie Reader
Contemporary Biography

Abigail Breslin
Aly and AJ
Ashley Tisdale
Charles Schulz
David Archuleta
Drake Bell & Josh Peck
Dylan & Cole Sprouse
Emma Watson
Jamie Lynn Spears
Jimmie Johnson
Jordin Sparks
Larry Fitzgerald
Miley Cyrus
Selena Gomez
Syd Hoff
Tom Brady

Albert Pujols
Amanda Bynes
Brenda Song
Dakota Fanning
Demi Lovato
Dr. Seuss
Eli Manning
Hilary Duff
Jennette McCurdy
Johnny Gruelle
Justin Bieber
LeBron James
Miranda Cosgrove
Shaquille O'Neal
Taylor Lautner
Tony Hawk

Alex Rodriguez
AnnaSophia Robb
Brittany Murphy
Dale Earnhardt Jr.
Donovan McNabb
Dwayne "The Rock" Johnson
Emily Osment
Jaden Smith
Jesse McCartney
Jonas Brothers
Keke Palmer
Mia Hamm
Raven-Symoné
Story of Harley-Davidson
Tiki Barber
Victoria Justice

Library of Congress Cataloging-in-Publication Data
Tracy, Kathleen.
  Justin Bieber / by Kathleen Tracy.
     p. cm. — (A Robbie reader)
  Includes bibliographical references and index.
  ISBN 978-1-58415-895-0 (library bound)
  1. Bieber, Justin, 1994– —Juvenile literature. 2. Singers—Canada—Biography—Juvenile literature. I. Title.
  ML3930.B416T73 2011
  782.42164092—dc22
  [B]

2010014900

ABOUT THE AUTHOR: Kathleen Tracy has been a journalist for over twenty years. Her writing has been featured in magazines including *The Toronto Star*'s "Star Week," *A&E Biography* magazine, *KidScreen*, and *TV Times*. She is also the author of over 85 books, including numerous books for Mitchell Lane Publishers, such as *The Fall of the Berlin Wall*; *Paul Cézanne*; *The Story of September 11, 2001*; *The Clinton View*; *We Visit Cuba*; *Demi Lovato*; and *Emma Watson*. Tracy lives in the Los Angeles area with her two dogs and African Grey parrot.

PUBLISHER'S NOTE: The following story has been thoroughly researched and to the best of our knowledge represents a true story. While every possible effort has been made to ensure accuracy, the publisher will not assume liability for damages caused by inaccuracies in the data, and makes no warranty on the accuracy of the information contained herein. This story has not been authorized or endorsed by Justin Bieber.

TABLE OF CONTENTS

Words in **bold** type can be found in the glossary.

Wherever Justin goes, fans follow! Justin is surrounded by fans during a February 2010 performance in Miami Beach for *The Early Show*.

Frenzied Fans

Being a teen idol can be risky! Ten days before Christmas in 2009, Justin Bieber was at a shopping mall near Los Angeles, California. He was there to perform a free outdoor concert. Radio Disney had urged fans to come and hear him sing. Thousands of them did.

Outside the mall, traffic was snarled with cars trying to find parking. The area where the concert was to happen was packed with people. Ten thousand fans, mostly girls, crowded into the **performance** (per-FOR-munts) area.

The fans farthest from the stage pushed forward, trying to get closer. Many of them

More than once, concerts have been canceled or cut short because of overly rowdy fans. "I'm a really **claustrophobic** [klos-truh-FOH-bik] person to begin with," Justin admits. "So it's very definitely scary when girls are all around me and I can't go anywhere."

were excitedly screaming for Justin. The concert was delayed for an hour while Radio Disney **officials** (oh-FIH-shuls) struggled to calm the crowd down. They didn't want anyone to get hurt. They also didn't want Justin to get mobbed by overly excited fans.

This wasn't the first time one of Justin's appearances nearly caused a riot. A month earlier, in November, he was supposed to visit a mall in New York. Some fans camped out overnight to see him. Three thousand fans showed up. While waiting for him to arrive, they started pushing each other. Five people ended up going to the hospital. To make sure nobody else got hurt, police canceled Justin's appearance.

In Los Angeles, the crowd finally settled down, but Justin was able to sing only a couple of songs before the fans went crazy again. Several girls in the crowd were hurt, so the concert was stopped. Fortunately, nobody was badly injured.

It seems that everywhere Justin goes, fans go wild. What a difference a year can make.

After his parents divorced, Justin lived with his mother in Stratford, Ontario. His mother, Pattie Bieber, helped Justin post his first video on YouTube.

North of the Border

Justin Drew Bieber was born in Stratford, Ontario (on-TAYR-ee-oh), Canada, on March 1, 1994. His parents, Jeremy and Pattie, separated when he was two years old. Jeremy eventually moved over a thousand miles away to Winnipeg, Manitoba. Justin stayed with his mother in Stratford, about 90 miles west of Toronto.

Justin has always been musical. He started playing the drums as a toddler. "My mom bought me my first drum kit when I was four, because I was banging on everything around the house, even couches," he told the *Khaleej*

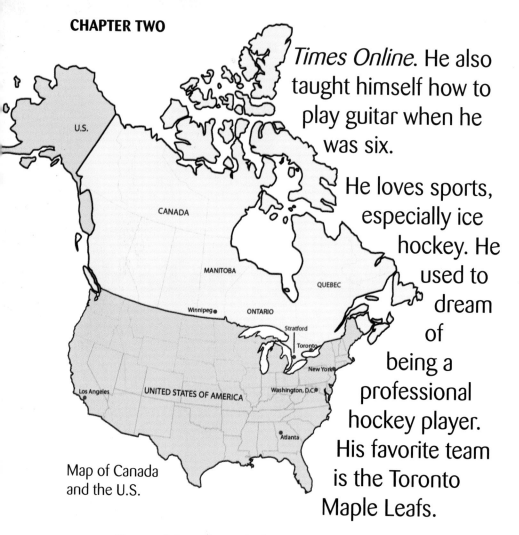

Times Online. He also taught himself how to play guitar when he was six.

He loves sports, especially ice hockey. He used to dream of being a professional hockey player. His favorite team is the Toronto Maple Leafs.

Map of Canada and the U.S.

One thing he didn't like was school. Classmates bullied Justin because he was short for his age. He did not have many friends, so he spent a lot of time playing sports or playing music.

As he practiced his instruments, he would also sing. He enjoyed both dance songs and

Justin was excited to throw the first pitch before a baseball game between the Chicago White Sox and the Kansas City Royals in May 2010. His real love is hockey, though. He still plays whenever his schedule allows.

ballads (BAL-ids). Even though his mother worked, there was never much money. To help her out, Justin sometimes sang as a **street performer** to bring in extra money.

Justin shows off his drumming skills during an appearance at a New Zealand school. Born with natural music talent, he got his first drum kit when he was four years old. He taught himself how to play the guitar when he was six years old.

When Justin was twelve, he entered a singing **competition** (kom-peh-TIH-shun) called Stratford Idol. He says he did it just for fun. He performed the Matchbox Twenty song "3 A.M." Justin didn't win—but he came in second place. He was thrilled!

"Some of my **relatives** [REH-lih-tivs] who couldn't make it wanted to see how I did," he recalled to *Billboard*. Justin and his mother posted a video of him singing on YouTube. He wanted his relatives to be able to watch it. They could not have dreamed what happened next.

Justin plays a Fender DG-21S acoustic guitar.

In December 2009, Justin was invited to perform in a Christmas show in Washington, D.C. "I have a house in Stratford and I got a house in Atlanta but I don't really live anywhere," he says. "I live on the road. I'm kind of like living in a suitcase, traveling so much."

YouTube Sensation

Until he entered the talent contest, few people knew Justin could sing. Even when he posted the video of his performance on YouTube, he didn't tell his school mates or friends.

"They knew me for playing sports," he explained to *Billboard*. "I just wanted to be a regular kid, and I knew they wouldn't treat me the same way if I told them."

Justin and his mother noticed that the number of people watching the YouTube clip kept growing. They knew that people other than his family must be watching his video. "I was like, 'Well, I don't have a hundred people in my family,'" Bieber told *The Boston Globe*.

"Then I was like, 'I don't have 500 people in my family.'" The number of views just kept going up.

Inspired, Justin made more home videos to post online. He sang songs by Usher, Ne-Yo, and Stevie Wonder. Each time he did, more and more people watched. Chris Brown even

Usher was impressed by Justin's talent. For Justin's sixteenth birthday, Usher bought him a Range Rover.

contacted him! Brown called to say how much he enjoyed Justin's video of his song "With You."

After seven months, Justin had gotten more than 50 million views of his videos. He was a true YouTube **sensation** (sen-SAY-shun). One of the people who checked him out was Scott "Scooter" Braun. Braun was a former record **executive** (ek-ZEH-kyoo-tiv) turned talent manager. He had discovered rapper Asher Roth. Now he was interested in Justin!

Braun lives in Atlanta, Georgia. He flew Justin and his mother in for a meeting. It was the first time Justin had ever been on an airplane. While in Atlanta, Braun introduced Justin to Usher. Justin Timberlake was also interested in working with Bieber. In October 2008, Justin Bieber signed a record deal with Usher and Island Records.

A short time later, Justin and his mother moved to Atlanta. Their lives were about to change forever.

Justin sings to a fan during the Pepsi Super Bowl Fan Jam in February 2010. He says he's a romantic at heart. "A girl has to have a beautiful smile, beautiful eyes, and she should have a good sense of humor. She should be honest, loving, and trustworthy."

Biebermania

As soon as he arrived in Atlanta, Justin began recording his first album. In May 2009, his first single, "One Time," was released. The song peaked at number 17 on Billboard's Hot 100. It reached number 12 on the Canadian Hot 100. Within six months, the music video for "One Time" had been viewed more than 17 million times on YouTube.

Usher also appears in the video. Justin told the *Vancouver Sun* about Usher: "He's like a big brother to me. We just hang out and don't really talk about music a lot. We go go-karting and to arcades and movies."

Justin hangs out with Beyoncé and her nephew Daniel Julez J. Smith at the 2010 Grammys. Justin admits, "I have crushes, but they're all too old. Like Beyoncé—she has a husband, I might get shot!"

Justin admitted to the *Stratford Beacon Herald* that he missed his friends in Canada. "But I kind of like the big city," he said of Atlanta. When he had time, Justin played hockey on a local Atlanta team. After the release of his single, though, **promoting** (pruh-MOH-ting) his music took all his time.

Sometimes he would be a guest on radio shows. Many radio stations are located in office buildings, so going to these **interviews** (IN-ter-vyoos) was stressful for Justin. It wasn't because he was shy. Instead, he told *Girls' Life*, "I'm very **claustrophobic** [klos-truh-FOH-bik] and scared of elevators."

Justin released three more singles on iTunes during the summer and autumn of 2009. The songs were "One Less Lonely Girl," "Love Me," and "Favorite Girl." He became the first solo artist to have four songs place in Billboard's Top 40 before the album is released.

Justin's album, called *My World*, was released on November 17, 2009. It debuted at number 7 on the Billboard 200 album chart.

Justin performs at a Nickelodeon event. He admits the constant traveling can be hard, but adds, "It doesn't really matter where I am as long as I have family and friends close to me. It's really all that matters."

In addition to singing, Justin also helped write songs for the album. "Most are about love and stuff that girls can **appreciate** [uh-PREE-shee-ayt]," he described to *Reuters* news service.

"I also co-wrote a song called 'Down to Earth.' It's a ballad about the feelings I had about my parents splitting up and how I helped my family get through it. A lot of kids have had their parents split up, and they should know that it wasn't because of something they did."

Justin adds to *MTV*, "Real life isn't perfect, so my album kind of portrays that. You just have to make the best of what you have. I hope people can relate to it."

When Justin turned fifteen in March 2009, he knew he looked much younger than his age. Usher and his manager hired a special coach to help with his image.

"I have a swagger coach that helps me and teaches me different swaggerific things to do," Justin told the *Examiner*, laughing. "He has helped me with my style and just putting different pieces [of clothing] together and being able to layer and stuff like that."

It obviously worked. Everywhere Justin goes, mobs of screaming fans follow. And Biebermania just keeps on growing.

Justin participated in Jumpstart's 4th annual National Read for the Record Day. Justin says he would like to start his own charity one day soon.

Looking Forward

Justin traveled all over the United States to promote "One Time" and his album. In addition to performing mall concerts, he was also a guest on radio and television shows. Meanwhile, he has had to keep up with his schoolwork (he is homeschooled).

"It has been overwhelming," he admitted to the *Timmins Times* in 2009. "I have a full-time job at fifteen—I love it."

His mother says Justin's days are so full that he's often exhausted. "He gets tired but keeps his spirits up."

In December 2009, Justin performed at the White House for President Barack Obama and First Lady Michelle Obama. The Christmas in Washington concert raised money for the National Children's Medical Center. He also sang with dozens of other performers in a remake of the song "We Are the World." The song was recorded to benefit victims of an **earthquake** (ERTH-kwayk) in Haiti (HAY-tee).

He also got to sing with Taylor Swift at the 2009 Jingle Ball in New York City. Justin is openly in awe of Swift. "It's not only that she's a great artist," he told *Girls' Life*. "She's just a very sweet girl. She's good to her fans and to her mom."

He also traveled with Taylor on a two-tour trip to Great Britain. And he returned to Canada for five solo concerts.

Despite his hectic schedule, Justin makes time for his fans on Facebook and Twitter. "I think the Internet is the best way to reach your fans," he told *Billboard*.

Justin performed with Celine Dion, Joe Jonas, and others on the 2010 "We Are the World 25 Years for Haiti" recording. He was honored to sing the first words of the song.

He admitted to *Girls' Life* in 2009 that he was too busy for a girlfriend. "I've only had a couple girlfriends, and haven't gotten too serious, but I look for girls with a good personality who can make me laugh. And I like taking a girl out for dinner and buying her flowers." Justin recalled one time when he took a girl out. "I got spaghetti and meatballs, which wasn't a smart thing to do. I spilled it all over me. She never went out with me again."

For the time being, Justin is happy to focus on his career. "I'm on the road constantly," the told the *Stratford Beacon Herald*. "I haven't been in one place for more than three days. But it's all worth it."

His fans couldn't agree more.

CHRONOLOGY

1994 Justin Drew Bieber is born in Stratford, Ontario, Canada, on March 1.

1996 His parents, Jeremy and Pattie, separate.

1998 Justin gets his first drum set.

2007 He enters Stratford Idol, a talent contest, and posts a video of his performance on YouTube.

2008 He signs with Island Records. He and his mother move to Atlanta, Georgia.

2009 His first single, "One Time," is released in May. His debut album, *My World*, is released in November. He performs for President and First Lady Obama at the White House for a Christmas benefit.

2010 He sings with eighty other performers on the benefit song "We Are the World 25 for Haiti." His second album, *My World 2.0*, hits the number 1 spot on the Billboard chart. He goes on a solo tour. Justin and *Karate Kid* star Jaden Smith appear in the video for "Never Say Never" from the movie's sound track. Justin wins four Teen Choice Awards and an MTV Video Music Award for Best New Artist. He appears as Jason McCann on *CSI: Crime Scene Investigation.* Paramount Pictures plans a 3-D movie about Justin's life, and he makes a deal with HarperCollins to publish his memoirs.

DISCOGRAPHY

Singles

2010 "Baby" (featuring Ludacris)
"Eenie Meenie" (with Sean Kingston
"Never Let You Go"
"Never Say Never" (featuring Jaden Smith)
"U Smile"
"Somebody to Love"

2009 "One Time"
"One Less Lonely Girl"
"Love Me"
"Favorite Girl"

Albums

2010 *My World 2.0*

2009 *My World*

FIND OUT MORE

Books

Rowlands, Millie. *Justin Bieber: Our World*. London: Orion, 2010.

Tieck, Sarah. *Justin Bieber: Singing Sensation*. Edina, MN: Buddy Books, 2010.

Works Consulted

"Bieber Concert Goes Crazy in Commerce." *EGP News Service*, December 17, 2009.

Bream, Jon. "Tweens Go Gaga for Justin Bieber." *Minneapolis Star Tribune*, December 11, 2009, p. D2.

Caramanica, Jon. "20-Year-Old Fogy Cedes Audience to 15-Year-Old." *New York Times*, December 14, 2009, p. C1.

Cluff, Paul. "Justin Bieber the Toast of the Town." *The [Stratford] Beacon Herald*, May 7, 2009. http://www.stratfordbeaconherald.com/ArticleDisplay.aspx?archive=true&e=1557965

"GL's Crushin' On . . . Justin Bieber." *Girls' Life*, December 1, 2009. http://www.highbeam.com/doc/1G1-213527994.html

Herrera, Monica. "Biebermania to Hit Allstate." *Chicago Sun-Times*, December 12, 2009, p. 25.

McGrath, Kristin. "The 'World' Is Already Teen Heartthrob's Oyster." *USA Today*, December 21, 2009, p. 6D.

Richards, Chris. "Justin Bieber, Elfin Face of a White House Christmas." *Washington Post*, December 20, 2009, p. E1.

"Tween Justin Bieber Fans Lose Control at NY Mall." *AP Online*, November 21, 2009. http://abcnews.go.com/Entertainment/wireStory?id=9144737

Vena, Jocelyn. "Justin Bieber Says My World Is 'Not Just About Love.'" *The Daily Gazette*, November 17, 2009.

Vena, Jocelyn, with reporting by Eric Ditzian. "Justin Bieber 'Remarkable' on 'We Are The World,' Director Says." *MTV.com*, February 12, 2010. http://www.mtv.com/news/articles/1631816/20100212/bieber_justin.jhtml

On the Internet

Justin Bieber Official Web Site
http://www.justinbiebermusic.com/

Justin Bieber's Facebook Page
http://www.facebook.com/JustinBieber?v=app_2347471856

Justin Bieber's MySpace Page
http://www.myspace.com/justinbieber

GLOSSARY

appreciate (uh-PREE-shee-ayt)—To feel thankful or grateful.

ballad (BAL-id)—A love song.

claustrophobic (klos-truh-FOH-bik)—Afraid of small spaces.

competition (kom-peh-TIH-shun)—An event in which two or more opposing sides try to win a challenge.

earthquake (ERTH-kwayk)—The sudden, strong movement of a large area of land.

executive (ek-ZEH-kyoo-tiv)—One of the top managers in a company.

interview (IN-ter-vyoo)—A talk between a person who asks questions and another person who answers them.

official (oh-FIH-shul)—A person who makes sure people follow the rules.

performance (per-FOR-munts)—A show.

promoting (pruh-MOH-ting)—Trying to convince people to buy something.

relatives (REH-lih-tivs)—People in your family, including cousins, uncles, and others.

sensation (sen-SAY-shun)—The cause of a lot of excitement.

street performer (STREET per-FOR-mer)—Someone who makes money by giving shows to people walking by on the street.

swagger (SWAG-ur)—To walk with confidence.

PHOTO CREDITS: Cover, pp. 1, 14, 27—Kevin Mazur/WireImage/Getty Images; p. 4—Gustavo Caballero/WireImage/Getty Images; p. 6—Alexander Tamargo/Getty Images; pp. 8, 20—Larry Busacca/Getty Images; p. 11—Ron Vesely/MLB Photos via Getty Images; p. 12—Sandra Mu/Getty Images for Tourism NZ; p. 16—Theo Wargo/WireImage for Clear Channel Radio New York/Getty Images; p. 18—Troy Rizzo/Getty Images; p. 22—Bryan Bedder/Getty Images for Nickelodeon; p. 24—AP Photo/Richard Drew. Every effort has been made to locate all copyright holders of materials used in this book. Any errors or omissions will be corrected in future editions of the book.

INDEX